Generously Donated by the Goodwyn Institute

MEMPHIS LIBRARY FOUNDATION

INSIDE THE INDUSTRY
PUBLISHING

BY BETH TOWNSEND

INSIDE THE INDUSTRY
PUBLISHING

BY BETH TOWNSEND

Content Consultant
Professor Jane Kinney-Denning
Director of Internships and Corporate Outreach
MS in Publishing Program, Pace University, New York, NY

ABDO
Publishing Company

CREDITS

Published by ABDO Publishing Company, 8000 West 78th Street, Edina, Minnesota 55439. Copyright © 2011 by Abdo Consulting Group, Inc. International copyrights reserved in all countries. No part of this book may be reproduced in any form without written permission from the publisher. The Essential Library™ is a trademark and logo of ABDO Publishing Company.

Printed in the United States of America,
North Mankato, Minnesota
112010
012011

Editor: Mari Kesselring
Copy Editor: David Johnstone
Interior Design and Production: Emily Love
Cover Design: Emily Love

Library of Congress Cataloging-in-Publication Data
Townsend, Beth, 1975-
  Publishing / by Beth Townsend.
      pages cm. -- (Inside the industry)
  Includes bibliographical references.
  ISBN 978-1-61714-803-3
 1. Publishers and publishing--Vocational guidance--Juvenile literature.
2. Authorship--Vocational guidance--Juvenile literature. 3. Journalism-
-Editing--Vocational guidance--Juvenile literature. I. Title.
  Z278.T69 2011
  070.5023--dc22
                              2010042810

TABLE OF CONTENTS

Do you love to read? You might be suited for a career in publishing.

IS A PUBLISHING JOB FOR YOU?

"I love the printed word and have always appreciated the unique connection between author and reader."[1] —*Oprah Winfrey*

You read books and wonder how they are created. You even do some writing of your own. You enjoy reading fashion or sports magazines. You love the bright, colorful photographs and the interesting articles. Or, perhaps, you dream about visiting every state in the United States, or every country in Europe. You like to write about what you experience when you travel. Or, maybe you want to help an author sell the next big novel to a movie studio. You can accomplish any of these goals with a career in the publishing field.

SEE YOUR FUTURE

Pick up your favorite book. Of course, you know the author's name and maybe the publisher's, too. But, who else was involved in creating that one book? Chances are, a lot of people were behind the publication of the book, including editors, designers, marketing people, publishers, agents, and the people operating the printing press. Are you interested in the actual production of books or magazines? Not everyone is suited for every job in the publishing industry. You need to find the publishing job that is right for you.

If you like to read or even find errors in your textbook, becoming an editor may be the job for you. But, even the term *editor* covers a variety of jobs.

HUNDREDS OF OPTIONS

What types of products will you work with if you choose a career in publishing? Most people immediately think of publishing books, magazines, newspapers, and Web sites. However, these are not the only things that are published. For example, publishers create calendars and planners. Some publishers might create pamphlets for businesses.

Pick up your favorite magazine and look through it. The glossy pages catch your eye. The layout looks interesting, but you think of different ways it could be arranged. Behind every magazine is a magazine editor. At large magazines, the executive editorial staff oversees the editorial direction. These people are executive editors. Perhaps you would like to become an editor in chief of a magazine. You may have to start at the bottom as an editorial intern or editorial assistant. A lot of hard work and determination can get you to the top. Do you know a lot about computers? Have you built your own Web site? These days, many magazines are published exclusively on the Internet or have online components to complement their print versions. Understanding technology is an important part of making it in the publishing field.

"We must go beyond textbooks, go out into the bypaths and untrodden depths of the wilderness and travel and explore and tell the world the glories of our journey."[2]

—John Hope Franklin, author and law professor at Duke University

Maybe you're the kind of person who is always writing in a journal. In that case, you may be better suited to being a writer than an editor. But what kind of writer? You could be a journalist, a travel writer, or even a novelist.

Writers and editors encompass the creative side of publishing, but there is also the business side. Book publishers and agents work in this area. Book publishers are usually in charge of an entire publishing house. They are responsible for the budget, oversee the staff, and decide what types of material their company will publish. Book publishers work with editors, graphic designers, and a marketing team. You may know that your favorite actor has an agent, but did you know that some authors have agents, too? Literary agents represent authors and are intermediaries between them and their publishing houses. Sometimes an agent helps an author sell the rights of his or her book to a movie studio.

WHERE SHOULD YOU LIVE?

If you choose to work in publishing, it may be wise to move to a larger city, such as New York City, Dallas, Texas, or San Francisco, California, where there are many large publishing houses. For some jobs, you may be able to work remotely as a freelancer.

LESS LITERARY CAREER PATHS

In addition to these jobs, some people in publishing work with the visual elements of publications. Graphic designers lay out the text in books, magazines, and newspapers. They might also create the design in which the text is placed. That means they create icons, borders, and other elements you see on the page, but they might never actually read the whole book. Web designers might create Web sites for a publication. Often, an art director oversees several designers at a publishing house and makes final decisions about design elements.

Graphic designers create unique designs for publications.

Most big publishing houses also have a marketing division. The people who work in marketing are experts on what people like to buy and why. They do their best to make sure the company is producing material that will sell to many customers. People in marketing also decide the best way to promote the material.

All these jobs work together to create the final printed product that shows up at your library or in your mailbox. There are many ways to be involved in this fast-paced and ever-changing field.

TEN POPULAR PUBLISHING JOBS

Are you ready to explore which publishing jobs are good fits for you? This book will cover the following jobs in depth: a magazine editor, a book publisher, a literary agent, and a travel writer. But first, here is a list of other popular jobs in the field.

1. Editorial assistant: Assistants can be found in all of the departments in a publishing house, including marketing assistants, production assistants, and publicity assistants. While at the bottom of the totem pole in a publishing house, editorial assistants play an important part in the publishing industry. They handle the day-to-day office tasks such as letter writing, filing, answering phones, and keeping their editor organized.

NEW PUBLISHING TECHNOLOGY

As the world has become more reliant on technology, many industries have changed drastically, including publishing. With the inventions of the iPad, the Kindle, and the Nook, more publishers are creating material that is available electronically, in the form of e-books, to be used on these devices, called e-readers. In fact, some books are only published in e-book form. Marketing people at publishing houses also commonly use electronic tools such as social networking sites to promote newly published materials.

2. Editor in chief: Holding a top position in a publishing house, the editor in chief has many duties, depending on the type of publication. He or she can be in charge of topic selection, scheduling, design, and layout.

3. Graphic designer: Graphic designers are important in many industries. In the publishing field, a graphic designer may be responsible for designing ads, book layouts, article layouts, and more. In some book publishing companies, the graphic designer lays out the books and, most important, designs book covers.

4. Sales and marketing staff: These people are chiefly responsible for selling or increasing sales of magazines, newspapers, and books.

5. Author: Either on assignment or working from his or her own inspiration, the author writes books, articles, blogs, and more.

6. Web designer: A Web designer is not specific to the publishing industry. However, many magazines, newspapers, and book publishers have Web sites that need to be designed and updated. In fact, some publications appear only on Web sites. Web designers create the look and organization of a Web site.

7. Proofreaders, copy editors, and fact checkers: Proofreaders give text a quick but thorough review for grammar, spelling, and other errors. Copy editors make sure the text reads smoothly and that style

Photographers may be hired to take specific photographs for a publication.

choices, such as the use of hyphens or capitalization, are consistent throughout. Fact checkers make sure all dates, statistics, and other facts in the publication are correct.

8. **Assistant or associate agent:** In some larger literary agencies, a person starts as an assistant or associate agent. He or she may have all the same duties as an agent but may not take on as many clients. When an assistant or associate agent gains enough experience, he or she could be promoted to agent.

9. **Photographer:** Newspapers, magazines, and book publishers usually use photographs in their publications. Sometimes a photographer may be called to photograph specific subjects. The majority of photographers are self-employed.

10. **Art director:** Some publications have an art director. The art director oversees the graphic designers and their layout and design of the publication.

The publishing industry holds abundant opportunities for career paths. Read on to find out how you can become a part of it.

Being able to communicate well with others is an important skill for any publishing career.

There are two types of magazines—trade and general interest.

WHAT IS A
MAGAZINE EDITOR?

Magazines are a great way to find out information on your favorite sport, the latest fashion styles, celebrity gossip, news, and more. Some magazines are released monthly, while others hit the stands every week. Some come out only four times a year. Most magazines created today are available in both print and online formats. Think about your favorite magazines. Chances are a magazine editor worked hard to help make it great.

A magazine is a type of periodical. There are three types of periodicals: journals, newspapers, and magazines. Journals usually circulate in the academic or professional world. Journals consist of essays and studies by professors, researchers, and professionals in the field the journal covers. There are many popular journals for different subjects, including medical journals such as *The Journal of American Medical Association* and *The New England Journal of Medicine*, scientific journals such as *Science*, or literary journals such as *Zone 3* and *Colorado Review*.

Newspapers, such as the *New York Times* and *Washington Post*, provide stories on current events. Some newspapers focus on local news while others report events

OLDEST MAGAZINE?

One of the oldest magazines in the world still in publication is *The Scots Magazine*. It was first published in 1739. This magazine is based in Scotland and highlights Scottish life. The magazine includes general interest articles, book reviews, and music reviews. The online version of the magazine contains games and trivia.

from around the world. Newspapers may be available on Web sites or in print form. Some people still have a newspaper delivered to their front door.

Magazines, on the other hand, differ from journals and newspapers in both appearance and content. While journals and newspapers usually have mostly text on the inside, magazines tend to have many images and an attention-catching cover. There are two types of magazines: trade magazines and general interest magazines. Trade magazines, such as *Public Management* and *Advertising Age*, are more professional. They give information about a specific industry or profession. Advertisements in trade magazines are usually light and often relate to the subject of the magazine. General interest magazines, such as *People*, *Bridal Guide*, *Women's Day*, and *Time*, are more likely meant to entertain the reader. General interest magazines usually have many advertisements that run along the side of the page, on full pages, and on back covers. No matter what type of magazine you like, there is a team working to make it the best magazine possible.

DIFFERENT SECTIONS

Did you know that one magazine may have different sections? Some magazines have book, movie, and song reviews. Other magazines may have a recipe section or a place where readers can write in with their opinions. Each section may have a team, including a magazine editor, working together on it. Check out your favorite magazine to see whether you can spot the different sections.

Many people are involved in the creation of a magazine—advertisers, photographers, marketers, and more. The editorial team is in charge of the magazine's words. They also have a say in how the words combine with the magazine's visual elements. This team comprises many levels. From highest to lowest, it may consist of managing editors, associate editors, assistant editors, editorial assistants, and editorial interns. A magazine editor may fit into any of these positions. Check the masthead of your favorite magazine to see a list of the different editorial job titles.

A magazine editor may be in charge of several articles in a magazine or, if he or she is the editor in chief, the entire publication. He or she must work hard to meet deadlines. That means being organized enough to keep track of many projects. A magazine editor might have a say in the plan of the magazine, often choosing topics for articles that fit its aim. To do this, a good understanding of the publication's intended audience is imperative.

THE HOOK

Did you know that some magazines require a "hook" for each article? The hook, or the piece's opening text, is written in a way that draws the reader in. Open your favorite magazine, and go to one of the articles. Is the first paragraph exciting? Did it make you want to read the rest of the article? If so, that's a good hook.

A magazine editor works to ensure the high quality of the text in print and on the magazine's Web site. That includes checking for grammar, spelling, and punctuation errors. But it also means making sure the articles are well organized and logical, interesting, and fun to read. Along with the other editors, the magazine editor helps the art director find

Janet Ozzard is a magazine editor in New York.

photographs, illustrations, and other artwork to complement an article.

Working with writers is one of the most important and challenging parts of being a magazine editor. When assigning an author to write an article, the magazine editor must be very clear about the intent of the article, its length, and its audience. Once the author submits the article, the real work begins. The magazine editor must check that the author's article meets the requirements outlined at the beginning of the project. Furthermore, changes may need to be made to the article if the author did not follow directions or if the magazine requires a different slant on the topic than originally planned for. Through e-mail, phone conversations, and face-to-face meetings, the editor will work with the author to revise the article. In some cases, the editor may even rewrite parts of the article without the author's help.

WHAT IS A MAGAZINE EDITOR'S WORK ENVIRONMENT?

Most magazine editors work in offices. They usually spend several hours a day editing articles and answering e-mails on a computer. A magazine editor might also edit on hard copy, or printouts, of the magazine. These are called page proofs. Magazine editors also often attend meetings with other editors and designers who help create the publication. They might work together to brainstorm for upcoming issues. They may also need to approve photographs or illustrations to be used with their articles.

Many magazine editors work in big cities. They may travel occasionally to attend conferences, but the job requires little travel. Some magazine editors might work as freelance magazine editors at home and away from the company's offices.

Some work environments may be fast paced and high-pressure; others may be a bit relaxed. Magazines need to put out the most current information. Articles may change at the last minute depending on what is happening in the world. But all magazines, whether trade or general interest, have deadlines that need to be met. Some of these deadlines may be very tight. A missed deadline can mean a loss of time and money for the magazine. The office may be tense as deadlines near, and all teams are working hard to put the magazine together. A magazine editor often works on several articles at once. He or she must keep track of each and keep it on schedule, which is another reason why organizational skills are so important for this position.

HOW IS THE JOB MARKET FOR MAGAZINE EDITORS?

As of 2010, the job outlook for magazine editors was fair. Jobs for magazine editors were expected to rise about 8 percent by 2018.[1] Jobs for book and magazine editors can expect a similar rate. However, as more magazines become available on the Internet, it is important to keep up with the current technological trends. Some magazines now publish only online. Some magazines that publish in print are moving to an online format. Other magazines have a print form and maintain a Web site with supplemental information. With only approximately 129,600 editors employed for all publications as of 2008, competition for editing jobs is high.[2] Prospective magazine editors need to be skilled and resolute to land a job.

As of 2009, the average salary for an editor ranged between $28,430 and $97,360 a year.[3] The salary may depend on the type of magazine the editor works for. Most editors make approximately $50,800.[4] A beginning editor will also make closer to the lower figure, but with a lot of hard work, lower-level editors can work their way to a position as magazine editor and obtain a salary increase. Although a job as a magazine editor is neither high paying nor easy to obtain, if you really love magazines and editing, it will be worth the challenges you will face.

David Granger is the editor in chief of *Esquire* magazine.

A PROFILE OF
A MAGAZINE EDITOR

Lisa Patterson is the editor in chief at Premier Media Group in Tacoma, Washington, and has been a magazine editor for four years. Patterson oversees two publications, *South Sound* magazine and 425 magazine. The magazines are mainly general interest, high-quality, glossy magazines. When asked whether her magazines are also online, Patterson explained, "We do have Web sites for both titles, but our main focus is the print editions at this time."[5]

Patterson was a newspaper reporter for several years and freelanced for magazines, including with the company she works for now. She enjoyed writing for magazines because she was able to cover interesting and inspiring stories. Patterson likes that magazines are visual and that she can use art, photography, and design to make written words more inviting. As an editor, she likes to help other writers, graphic designers, and photographers showcase their talents in the publications.

Patterson has a long journalism background. "I studied journalism young," she said. "I even wrote for my elementary school newspaper called *The Bearly News*. (Teddy bears were our mascot!) I have always loved writing and also wrote for my high school and college newspapers. I earned my bachelor's degree in media at Pacific Lutheran University in Tacoma and interned in college at a couple of news publications."[6]

Patterson thinks the best magazine editors are writers first. She recommends taking a lot of writing classes and English courses. She also suggests taking a public relations course because magazine editors often work with public relations people. Patterson thinks a couple of business courses would also be helpful because, as an editor, you are also often a manager. Photography, graphic design, and other arts-related courses will help you be an editor who appreciates not only the words but also the artistic side of magazines.

Patterson says, "My job is exciting and fun, especially when the magazine comes back from the printer, and you can see all your hard work paid off in a beautiful way."[7]

A DAY IN THE LIFE OF A MAGAZINE EDITOR

A magazine editor's day is usually very busy. Many magazine editors have to answer e-mails and return phone calls from their coworkers, current and prospective authors, and many others every morning. They also need to communicate with their team to keep their deadlines on track. These day-to-day tasks require a lot of time.

A magazine editor has meetings to attend and future issues to help plan, too. Depending on the publication and their position, magazine editors may need to meet with advertisers to discuss upcoming advertisements, whether the magazine is online or in print. A magazine editor often meets with writers and photographers to talk about new assignments and ideas, too. Meeting with public relations people can also be a daily activity.

A magazine editor has to make sure interviews and articles are accurate and quoted correctly. In some cases, a magazine editor may need to obtain permission to include an interview, recipe, book excerpt, song lyric, poem, or other work in the magazine. A magazine editor also spends a fair amount of time editing articles and brainstorming article ideas with the editorial team.

BRAINSTORM!

Brainstorming is an important part of a magazine editor's day. The editor and his or her staff meet to brainstorm ideas for upcoming issues. They may brainstorm about article ideas, photographs, ads, and more. Once an idea is approved, the magazine editor and the team get to work. You can practice brainstorming right now! Brainstorm with your friends about what to do on the weekend. Throw out different ideas, and write them down. Make sure your friends contribute to the conversation, but encourage everyone to be realistic about their suggestions.

TOP FIVE QUESTIONS ABOUT BECOMING A MAGAZINE EDITOR

1. *What skills will I need to develop to become a magazine editor?*

    You'll need to develop writing, editing, time management, and communication skills.

2. *What type of education do I need to become a magazine editor?*

    You'll usually need a bachelor's degree from a university. Majors in journalism or English are especially desired.

3. *How much money will I make as a magazine editor?*

    This varies greatly by publication size and position. As of 2009, editor salaries ranged between $28,430 and $97,360 a year.[8]

4. *How do I know whether I'm good enough to be a magazine editor?*

    Is English one of your favorite classes? Do you do well on papers and other writing assignments? Do you like to read and write? If so, then editing may be the right career choice for you. Start practicing now! Ask to help edit your friends' or classmates' papers.

5. *How do I decide what type of magazine I want to work for?*

    You'll want to choose a magazine that covers something you are interested in. There are magazines

Fashion magazines such as *Bazaar* are one popular type of general interest magazine.

that cover all sorts of topics from fashion to travel and more. Being interested in the magazine's focus will make your job more fun and rewarding.

Editors must be organized and hardworking.

WOULD YOU MAKE A GOOD MAGAZINE EDITOR?

Do you think you would make a good magazine editor? If you like to read articles, look at photographs, plan ahead, and meet deadlines, becoming a magazine editor may be a good choice for you. However, there are more than just a few skills that would help you succeed as a magazine editor.

A KEEN EYE

A magazine editor needs to have a sharp eye and should be able to read articles thoroughly while assessing the content of the writing. You'll also need to be able to catch mistakes, such as spelling, grammar, and punctuation errors, in the text. Many magazine editors enjoy learning about grammar rules and how articles should be organized. It is fun for them to hunt for mistakes and correct them.

If you aren't familiar with grammar and punctuation rules, there is plenty of time to learn! Pick up a copy of *The Elements of Style* or *The Associated Press Stylebook*. These guides explain different grammar and punctuation rules. A magazine usually follows the rules in one of these books, most commonly *The Associated Press Stylebook*. You can get a jump start on your career by exploring these texts.

EDITOR IN CHIEF

Did you know that an editor in chief of a magazine could be in charge of more than one magazine? If one large corporation owns several magazines, that corporation may have one editor in chief to run all the magazines. However, if the magazines are large, then each publication would have its own editor in chief.

BE A "PEOPLE PERSON"

Being able to work with people is also very important for a magazine editor. Magazine editors work with many people— from those who are on their staff to freelancers, who work outside the office. Therefore, magazine editors use many forms of communication, including e-mail, telephone, and face-to-face interaction. Magazine editors need to be firm, direct, and professional with their requests when needed.

KNOW TECHNOLOGY

Being skillful with a computer is a must for a magazine editor. Magazine editors especially need to be comfortable with word processing, photo editing, and Web site building programs. If you enjoy learning about different computer programs and pick up on them quickly, you are in a good spot. To find out what programs you may need to know, try contacting your favorite magazine or one that you could see yourself working for. Tell them you are a student interested in becoming a magazine editor. Most likely, they will be happy to answer your questions.

STICK TO THE SCHEDULE

Other important skills for a magazine editor include time management and organizational skills. Remember that a magazine editor is in charge of keeping his or her projects on schedule. A magazine is usually printed on a specific day. If the magazine is late, it might not get printed at all, or it might arrive late to newsstands and subscribers' mailboxes.

It's not difficult to find out if you are good at managing your time. Do you keep lists of when your homework is due? Do you create a schedule to keep your assignments on track? Are you rarely late to meet a friend or turn in a homework assignment? Those are good habits to cultivate for your future as a magazine editor. If you don't have this skill yet, tracking your due dates for school projects can help you improve.

CHECKLIST

Check out this checklist to see if you're on the way to becoming a magazine editor.

- *Do you like English or journalism?*

- *Do you keep up with current events?*

- *Do you know how to use computer software for Web design or word processing?*

- *Do you like to read?*

- *Are you prepared to meet tight deadlines?*

- *Do you enjoy fast-paced environments?*

- *Can you communicate with people in an effective manner?*

If you answered yes to most of these questions, you could be on your way to a career as a magazine editor. But, even if you are unsure of your answers for the checklist, that doesn't

One way to prepare for a career as a magazine editor
is to develop your writing and editing skills.

mean you cannot become a magazine editor. If you want to be a magazine editor, do your best, and strive to achieve that goal.

HOW TO GET THERE

WRITE AND EDIT

If you have decided that becoming a magazine editor is the career for you, you can get started now! Does your school have a newspaper, magazine, or online blog? If it does, see how you can help. Offer to be a reporter, writer, or editor. You can learn a lot about how a publication operates. You will also have a chance to practice your writing and editing skills.

What if your school does not have any publications? See whether you can start one. Talk to the principal or a favorite English or journalism teacher. Ask your classmates whether they would be interested in being involved.

If starting a publication at your school isn't an option, don't give up yet! Make a magazine on your own. Use a computer to write your own articles and design your own magazine. Add photos, or even create your own advertisements. You can even get your friends involved. Practice being a magazine editor by setting deadlines that you'll need to work toward. Then, everyone can collaborate to put the magazine together. Working on a newspaper, magazine, or blog will give you valuable experience in not only writing and editing but also working with others.

STYLES

Good editors know how to edit and write. They may need to learn how to follow particular editing rules, or a style. Different styles come from style guides that describe them. Style guides help keep spelling, grammar, and other details consistent throughout a publication. Everyone working for a publication will use the same style. Some popular styles are *The Chicago Manual of Style*, *Modern Language Association* (MLA) style, *Associated Press* (AP) style, *American Psychological Association* (APA) style, and *American Medical Association* (AMA) style. Each has its own set of rules and a publication that explains those rules.

MAKE A PORTFOLIO

If you write for a newspaper, magazine, or blog, start your own portfolio. A portfolio is a collection of your writings, usually in a professional book or binder. When you go on interviews for internships or jobs, you'll take this portfolio with you. It's a great way to show employers you're serious about writing and editing. Be sure to include only your very best work.

EDUCATION

Take writing classes. If your school has certain language arts requirements, make sure you take those classes. If you can take electives, choose writing classes. The type of writing classes you decide to take depends on the career you choose. General classes such as journalism or creative writing are safe bets. Does your school offer a class on editing? If so, take that, too. It is also a good idea to take a Web site-building class if it is available.

Today, most magazine editors have a college degree in English or journalism. If you choose to become a magazine editor, consult with your guidance counselor or adviser to make sure you take the correct

BLOG IT!

Do you want to work for a magazine that caters to one topic, such as a fashion or sports magazine? With a trusted adult's permission, start your own online blog. Start writing articles about your favorite subject, and post them on the blog. Be sure to proofread carefully before you post—check for spelling and grammar errors.

classes. Your guidance counselor may also be able to help you research colleges that have strong English or journalism programs. You may also contact colleges you are interested in to see whether you can talk to either a student or a professor in the English or journalism program. Talking to a student especially will help you get an idea of whether this is the school you want to attend and the program for you.

INTERNSHIPS AND NETWORKING

Internships and networking are great opportunities to gain experience within the magazine field. Most internships are offered during the summer and are unpaid. Internships will help you learn the ropes in the magazine industry. If you can't find an internship at a local magazine, try finding one at a local newspaper or other print entity. Even helping your school or church with a weekly newsletter could be good experience for you. Ask your family and friends whether they know anyone who is in the magazine field. Maybe they can help you find an internship. If internships are

FOLLOW YOUR INTERESTS

There are magazines for all interests. If you want to work in magazine publishing, it can be great to work for a magazine on a topic you already enjoy. *Sports Illustrated* is the most popular sports magazine in the United States. Fashion magazines such as *ELLE*, *Vogue*, and *Glamour* highlight the many types of fashion, styles, and the hot new trends. There are also magazines that focus on cars, gardening, celebrities, fitness, weddings, literature, computers, photography, and more.

not available, or if you just don't have the time to devote to one right now, ask whether you can job shadow a magazine editor. Job shadowing will allow you to see firsthand what a magazine editor does every day. You should make sure to ask questions about the job. Job shadowing can also introduce you to people who work in the publishing industry. Making a good impression on these people is very important. You might be working with or for them one day. The more contacts like this that you have, the more likely one of these people will have an internship or job for you in the future.

Take these steps, and polish your skills. Don't be afraid to work hard, and don't give up! Before long, you could find yourself in your dream career.

Working as an intern in a magazine publishing office can give you valuable experience in magazine editing.

Book publishers help create books.

WHAT IS A BOOK PUBLISHER?

Book publishing is a large industry with many companies that specialize in fiction, nonfiction, children's books, graphic novels, textbooks, and more. One important position within a publishing company is that of the book publisher. This person oversees the editorial department, which acquires and edits text for publication. A book publisher helps a book move from manuscript form to a final, published copy, either print, electronic, or both. A book publisher likely worked in the publishing industry for a long time to work up to this managerial position.

Book publishers are the people at publishing houses who are responsible for overseeing everything it takes to turn a manuscript into a published book. That means he or she oversees choosing a manuscript to publish out of the many manuscripts literary agents and writers submit to the publishing house. Then, the book publisher supervises the production of turning a manuscript into a final book. This includes overseeing editing the manuscript as well as layout and cover design decisions. Finally, the book publisher works with the marketing department to decide how to promote the final product to buyers.

A book publisher may have started at the bottom of the publishing career as an intern or editorial assistant. Editorial assistants help the editors with day-to-day tasks, such as filing, making copies, and reading manuscripts. At a small publishing company, an editorial assistant might review first drafts of manuscripts, send manuscripts to copy editors and fact checkers, and input his or her own comments into the manuscript. As the editorial assistant gains experience, he or she can move up the ranks to assistant editor, associate editor, editor, senior editor, editor in chief, and finally, book publisher. Keep in mind that these titles and positions vary from company to company.

WHAT IS A BOOK PUBLISHER'S WORK ENVIRONMENT?

A book publisher's work environment depends on the size of the company that publisher works for. A book publisher usually works with editors and marketing people in a publishing house, which is a publisher's office. However, some book publishers start their own publishing companies out of their homes. Book publishers spend a lot of time in meetings and reviewing material to be published. Once they find a manuscript they feel fits the market, they help negotiate with the author or the author's agent to obtain rights to publish the material. Negotiations can be stressful and take a lot of a publisher's time. Depending on the publishing company, a book publisher might also be instrumental in deciding whether the book should be produced in print form, e-book form, or both and how it should be marketed. A book publisher's decisions are very important to the success of the book. Therefore, this job can be demanding.

HOW IS THE JOB MARKET FOR BOOK PUBLISHERS?

As of 2010, the job opportunities for book publishers were decreasing. However, this market might be changing with the emergence of digital media such as blogs and e-books. The book publisher must be aware of the market and its trends to keep on top of these changes. In 2008, the median salary for a book publisher was approximately $48,290 a year.[1] This salary

A book publisher might attend several meetings a day.

depends on the size of the publishing company. In a larger, well-known company, the salary could be higher.

A PROFILE OF A BOOK PUBLISHER

Michelle Bisson is a publisher with Marshall Cavendish Benchmark and has been a book publisher for eight years. Her publishing company publishes nonfiction books for school and public libraries. Bisson's imprint in particular publishes nonfiction series that are sold to libraries. An imprint is a subsection of the publishing company. Sometimes it is like a smaller company within the larger company. The imprint Bisson oversees also publishes e-books and has titles in the company's digital database.

Bisson has always been interested in editing and writing. For 20 years prior to becoming a children's book editor, she held many jobs, among them legal proofreader, production assistant at a nonprofit organization, medical editor for a scholarly journal, health and social issues reporter, book reviewer for a major newspaper, and medical writer for a nationally known publisher.

Bisson was hired as a "social issues" editor for an educational publisher. Then she became a senior editor at Marshall Cavendish. When the editorial director left to take another job shortly after she started at Marshall Cavendish, she volunteered to do a trial run as editorial director. Bisson did so well that she was given that job and then was promoted to publisher.

Bisson holds many degrees, including a bachelor's in English, a master of science in journalism, and a master of arts in psychology and counseling. For the publishing field, though, a bachelor's in English or journalism is usually required. Take classes

CHOOSING WHAT TO PUBLISH

Book publishers and their staff review a lot of manuscripts from authors who hope to be published. Some larger publishing companies have readers and assistants who go through stacks of submissions and read through the manuscripts. If they find one that seems publishable, they pass it on to an editor for further review. Book publishers also often look at manuscripts provided by literary agents. Some book publishers only accept manuscripts that come from literary agents, rather than allowing authors to submit work without the representation of an agent. Some manuscripts are chosen for publication. However, most authors receive rejection notices.

A book publisher might help editors with their projects and answer their questions.

in everything and anything that interests you. Bisson says, "The more you learn about the humanities and sciences and other subjects, the more you will bring to the table. As a nonfiction editor and publisher for the school library market, I work on books in all subject areas."[2]

Finding ideas for new books is a fun part of being a book publisher. When asked about how her company generates new book ideas, Bisson said, "We come up with the topics of our books through brainstorming meetings, ideas from our sales reps, librarians, and authors, from new authors, [and] from looking at the competition."[3]

Bisson offers a final great tip: "What you need to know about book publishing, you can learn on the job. One learns a job best by doing it; one learns about the world by experiencing it."[4]

A DAY IN THE LIFE OF A BOOK PUBLISHER

A book publisher may start a typical day by answering e-mails and phone calls from authors, editors, and other colleagues, but sometimes there is no set routine. The job can differ according to the many and varied tasks at hand. Also, some publishing companies work by season—books are usually published in the spring or fall. Depending on the season, the book publisher must make sure the books are ready to go to the printer on schedule.

MARKETING

While the book publisher is also an editor, it's a good idea for the publisher to have some business or marketing background. Sometimes, the publisher may be called into marketing meetings because he or she knows the most about the books being published for the upcoming season. The publisher can provide the marketing team with the specifics on the books for the season. This will help the marketing team to advertise correctly for the new books. Understanding what information will aid the marketing team is an important skill for a book publisher.

A book publisher must be able to stick to a schedule and meet deadlines.

The book publisher may spend time talking to editors about their assigned projects, helping them solve issues or questions. One of the most important things the book publisher does is make sure the editors and other staff meet deadlines.

Throughout the day and week, the book publisher attends several meetings. Ideas need to be brainstormed and approved. Up for discussion are titles of the books, schedules for new material, and sales and marketing plans for the upcoming publishing season.

Some book publishers also work on their own editorial projects. This means the publisher will read, critique, edit, choose photographs, and review designs for their project. Occasionally, the book publisher may talk to authors about continuing projects or new ideas.

TOP FIVE QUESTIONS ABOUT BECOMING A BOOK PUBLISHER

1. *What is the most important skill to have as a book publisher?*

   Possibly the most important skill for a book publisher to have is knowing how to read critically. The book publisher needs to know when a book is worth publishing. This means that he or she must understand the market and what people want to read. Mastering grammar and spelling, learning to be diplomatic, and writing clearly are also essential.

2. *What type of education do I need to become a book publisher?*

   Depending on the type of book publishing company you wish to work for, a bachelor's degree in English or journalism can help get you in the door. If you wish to work for a specialized publisher, such as one that focuses on history textbooks, then a bachelor's degree in history would be helpful. If your goal is to be a book publisher, editor in chief, or other high-up professional, a master's degree in publishing, English, or journalism would be beneficial.

3. *How much money will I make as a book publisher?*

   The salary for a book publisher depends on the company and the range varies in different states. For example, in 2010, a book publisher in Dallas, Texas, made an average of $42,000 a year while a book publisher in San Francisco, California, made approximately $55,000 a year.[5]

4. *How do I know whether I'm good enough to be a book publisher?*
    Since most book publishers get their start working as editors, you'll know within a few years whether being a book publisher is for you. If you like editing, reading, and writing, you might be good enough to be a book publisher. However, as a book publisher you will also need management skills and people skills.

5. *How do I decide what type of publisher to work for?*
    There are many types of publishers out there. What type of books are you interested in? If you like sports, find a company that produces books about sports. If you like fashion, work for a company that does a lot of fashion books. Larger companies may have more opportunities for growth, but smaller companies may expose you to more departments and responsibilities.

Book publishers must be able to guide and motivate others.

WOULD YOU MAKE A GOOD BOOK PUBLISHER?

Do you like to read? Would you be willing to learn how to edit and read critically? If so, then a career as a book publisher may be for you.

STARTING OUT

It is important for book publishers to have a lot of determination and an intense drive to succeed. Otherwise, they might never become a book publisher. Most book publishers start at the bottom of a company as editorial assistants. Working their way up can take many years of hard work in various positions.

Since a book publisher usually starts as an editorial assistant and then moves on to a position as an editor, a good book publisher will have already learned how to write well and how to spot grammar, spelling, and punctuation errors. An editor also reads for content and flow. This is important and helps ensure that the book makes sense and follows a logical order. Developing solid editing skills will be important if you plan to rise in the ranks and become a book publisher.

GUIDE AND MOTIVATE

A book publisher usually oversees the authors, editors, assistants, and interns. This means that he or she needs to have good communication and teaching skills. A book publisher needs

DEVELOP LEADERSHIP SKILLS

Good people skills are key to being a successful book publisher, and there are many ways you can develop them. Joining clubs in high school and college are great ways to start. Even better is to start a club at your school and serve as president. This will give you a true leadership experience.

to keep the editors and authors on track. Learning how to motivate people to reach high standards and complete their work on time is a valuable skill for a book publisher.

TECH SAVVY

Most publishing companies work on computers, so everything is digitized. Many companies also produce e-books. If you are interested in technology and e-book products, such as the iPad, the Kindle, and the Nook, you might already have some of the technology skills you'll need to develop as a book publisher. Knowledge of desktop publishing software, such as InDesign, is also a helpful skill.

THE CHECKLIST

Look over this checklist to see if you have what it takes to be a book publisher!

- *Do you like English or journalism?*

- *Do you have a strong background in computers? Are you familiar with word processing and design programs or other desktop publishing software?*

- *Do you like to read?*

- *Are you generally able to meet tight deadlines?*

- *Do you like working in fast-paced environments?*

- *Are you good with people?*

If you answered yes to most of these questions, you might be a good fit for a job as a book publisher. And, remember, even if you don't have the skills right now to become a book publisher, a lot of hard work and dedication will take you far. Don't give up.

HOW TO GET THERE

SELECT A FOCUS

To help you get started or to see whether book publishing is right for you, start reading! Do you like fiction? Nonfiction? Do you want to work for a fiction publisher, a nonfiction publisher, or one that publishes both types? Can you see yourself working on textbooks, novels, or children's picture books? It's okay if you cannot answer these questions yet. You might have to work with different types of books for a while before you decide which you like the best.

LEARN TO WRITE AND EDIT

Take writing classes. If your high school or a local college doesn't offer editing classes, see whether you can find an online class or an adult education class nearby. Check out your local library for books on editing and writing. You should get into the habit of writing something every day if you really want to improve your skills. Learning how to write well will help you spot good writing as a book publisher.

INTERNSHIPS AND NETWORKING

Send e-mails, or make calls to local publishing companies, asking whether they have internships available. If they don't,

Taking writing classes can help you spot good writing as a book publisher.

be positive and persistent, but not to the point of pestering, and maybe you'll be their first intern. Most interns don't get paid; they do it for the experience. But that experience will help you determine whether a career in book publishing is for you. Internships also look great on your résumé. An internship could also lead to possible employment within that company.

Networking is also important. Ask your family and friends whether they know anyone who works for a book publisher. Join blogs or forums that talk about publishing. E-mail publishing companies to see if you can conduct an informational interview with a book publisher. Let them know you're a student interested in the publishing field.

YOUR DEGREE

A bachelor's degree is required for most publishing jobs. Publishing companies look for degrees in English, journalism, or some sort of writing or literary field. If you are interested in going to a specialized book publisher (for example, a history book publisher),

PICK THE RIGHT PUBLISHER

As a book publisher, you may have to read manuscripts that have been submitted to your company but have nothing to do with the type of books your company publishes. This is a big pet peeve of some editors and publishers! While you are doing your own research for internships and jobs, make sure you know what types of books a company produces.

then you may want to have a degree in that field. As you progress in your publishing career, you may consider getting another bachelor's degree or a master's degree. Some larger companies may offer tuition reimbursement and thus help pay for schooling that will benefit your job.

One good rule of thumb is to research before you choose a major. Research job Web sites to see which degrees publishing companies value and often seek when screening job candidates.

Some colleges and universities offer a master's degree in publishing. It is likely a good idea to obtain a bachelor's degree first, then get experience in the book publishing field before committing to more schooling. A master's degree is not necessary to become a book publisher. However, if the field becomes more competitive, having an advanced degree may help you land a job. Plus, most master's programs in publishing also have strong internship programs, which are an important way to break into and gain experience in the industry.

PRACTICE!

Does your school have a newspaper, magazine, Web site, or blog? Be a part of that team. See whether they need editors. Becoming an editor of your school newspaper or newsletter will give you great experience not only in editing but also in working with people and meeting deadlines.

Practice your editing skills outside school by reading books or Web sites about editing and proofreading. Offer to read papers or letters written by your family and friends so you can edit them. Before you know it, you could be on your way to a career as a book publisher!

Starting a blog is a good way to gain writing and editing experience.

J. K. Rowling published her first book with the help of an agent.

WHAT IS A LITERARY AGENT?

Have you ever wondered how famous authors such as Stephen King, J. K. Rowling, or Stephenie Meyer get their work published? They have literary agents. Your favorite actors have agents, and authors have agents as well.

A literary agent acts as an author's representative to help the author obtain new contracts for writing books. In today's competitive market, most authors can only hope to publish their book with the help of an agent. An agent is an author's key to becoming published.

So, what exactly is it like to work as an agent? What does an agent do? Agents spend a lot of time reading manuscripts submitted by authors. By reading

> "You will love it and never want any other job. That's the way I feel."[1]
>
> —Kelly Sonnack, literary agent, Andrea Brown Literary Agency Inc.

a manuscript, they decide whether they will represent that author and his or her work. When a literary agent decides to represent an author, that means he or she will try to secure a publisher for that author's work. An agent must contact the author to either reject or accept his or her work. An agent rejects many more authors than he or she accepts. Writing rejection letters can be a difficult part of the job. The author who submitted work to the agent may be disappointed when it is rejected. However, the agent needs to be careful about whom he or she chooses to represent. The agent wants to represent an author who has work that will be interesting to a publisher. Publishers only publish work they believe will sell. The agent makes money only if the author's book is published.

After accepting a manuscript, the agent might ask the author to make changes before showing it to publishers.

The agent wants the manuscript to be in the best shape possible before he or she submits it. Literary agents already have connections with publishers. The agent knows the current publishing trends and knows what certain publishing companies are looking for. So, if the agent reads a manuscript that he or she thinks is very good, the agent can contact the right publishers directly to try to get the book published. The agent is the go-between for the publisher and the author. Often, the publisher and the author will never directly interact.

Once a publisher accepts a manuscript, the agent works out the terms of publication. The agent makes a percentage of what the author earns through book sales. Since the agent makes money from a commission, he or she works very hard to get the best deal with the publisher—the better the deal, the better the commission will be.

The agent may also have to negotiate the rights to a book or, simply put, whom the book belongs to. Sometimes a movie producer may want to turn a book into a film. The agent will handle the agreement and contract terms for the author.

Agents attend professional conventions, conferences, and seminars all over the country. These offer important networking opportunities. The agent could find contacts for new publishing companies or even a new author.

Agents often specialize in particular types of writing. For example, an agent might work only with poets or children's book authors. There are as many kinds of agents as there are types of books!

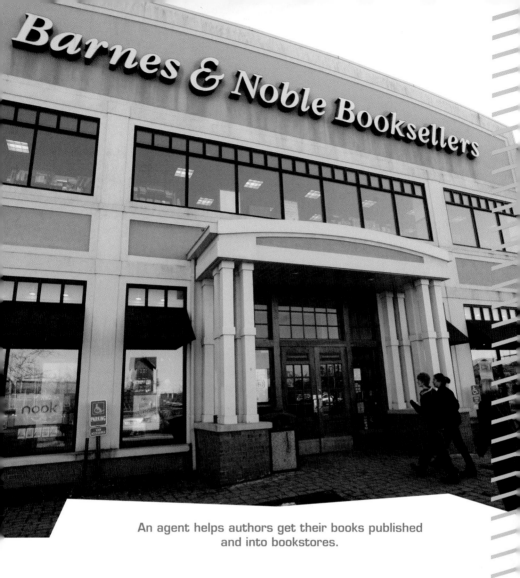

An agent helps authors get their books published and into bookstores.

WHAT IS A LITERARY AGENT'S WORK ENVIRONMENT?

An agent's work environment depends on whether the agent works for a large or small literary agency. Some agents own their own company and work for themselves. Other agents work at an agency with several agents. In a larger agency, the atmosphere may be competitive. There, agents strive to find the best authors and the next great book before their coworkers do. There can be competitiveness in a smaller agency, but it might not be as prominent. The agent might not spend a lot of time in his or her office if he or she needs to meet with authors and publishing companies.

A literary agent does a lot of reading. Some agents or agencies may have readers who read a large pile of material and pass along only the most interesting manuscripts to an agent. Between phone calls to editors and publishing companies, the agent must read manuscripts. He or she may also edit manuscripts and offer suggestions to the authors.

HOW IS THE JOB MARKET FOR LITERARY AGENTS?

Often, literary agents have worked in book publishing as editors before working as agents. Finding a job as a literary agent requires a lot of work and experience because there are not many jobs available. It takes a lot of talent and know-how to launch a successful agency. If you choose to become an agent, it may be wise to start with a well-established agency.

Since most agents work on a commission basis, compensation varies greatly. A literary agent in New York City makes approximately $63,000 a year.[2] However, a literary agent in Orlando, Florida, makes an average of $45,000 a year. So, on average, an agent could make around $50,000 a year.[3] Agents make most of their salary from commissions. That is, if they represent a book that sells well, they will make more money. Standard commissions for agents are approximately 10 to 15 percent of total book earnings.[4] In this very competitive field, the harder you work and the better your eye for recognizing great writing, the more money you could make.

A PROFILE OF A LITERARY AGENT

Andrea Brown is the president of Andrea Brown Literary Agency Inc. The agency has offices in San Francisco, California; San Diego, California; Los Angeles, California; and Chicago, Illinois. It has agents specializing in children's books. Although they do handle some adult nonfiction and fiction for clients who also write in those genres, they primarily focus on the children's book field.

Brown has a bachelor's degree in magazine journalism with minors in English and theater. She worked first for *Westchester* magazine and then got a job at Dell Publishing Company in the children's book department. Brown also worked at Random House with Dr. Seuss books and at Alfred A. Knopf with books

WILL YOU START YOUR OWN BUSINESS?

Some people may want to work for themselves or start their own agency. As with any business, people may want to work with someone who is experienced. So, if you start your own agency, it may take a while to develop a client list. It's a good idea to gain experience and industry connections first by working for an agency. Then, when you are comfortable and familiar with what an agent does, you can consider striking out on your own.

by Stan and Jan Berenstain. In 1981, she started her literary agency and was the first agent to specialize in both children's book authors and illustrators. Brown's agency has sold more than 2,000 titles to publishers. In 2010, her company had four *New York Times* bestsellers in the top ten slots.

Brown suggested, "People interested in this field would be wise to take children's literature classes, major in English or communications, and work for publishers or agents as interns. Reading a lot is crucial. They also should be technically savvy as e-books and other forms of producing content are becoming important."[5]

Brown noted that there is no typical day for an agent. She said that for almost 30 years, she has never been bored at her job. She explained, "Each day presents different issues, problems, excitement, and, maybe, the discovery

"I work a lot more than 40 hours a week because I am always serving my client list. I'm reading their books, submitting their projects to publishers, responding to offers and other requests, looking at contracts, advocating for subrights and foreign rights sales, and more. In addition to all that, I am always reading submissions from writers who hope to become clients."[7]

—*Mary Kole, associate agent, Andrea Brown Literary Agency Inc.*

of a brilliant new talent."[6] Brown offered this suggestion for a new agent: "An agent must multi-task, while staying focused and always, always put the client first. There are editors to meet, contracts to review, answers to questions from authors and illustrators, checks to issue, taxes to do, manuscripts to read and critique, and all kinds of paperwork, interviews to respond to, and writer's conferences to attend."[8]

Brown also mentioned that becoming an agent is not a fast way to make money. She explained that she always tells her new associates that it could take five to seven years to earn money as an agent on commission. "[B]ooks take years to sell, then possibly years to see published and earn back the advance payments, so it requires lots of patience and persistence."[8]

A DAY IN THE LIFE OF A LITERARY AGENT

For a literary agent, every day is different. Most will start the day by answering e-mails and phone calls. The e-mails could be from publishing companies or prospective authors. Agents spend a lot of time working out terms with their clients and publishers. An agent also must read a lot of manuscripts to find ones he or she believes would sell well.

An agent must spend some time keeping up his or her current contacts and trying to make some new ones. An agent often attends conventions, parties, and other business events to network with publishers and authors who are not yet represented. It is very important that an agent remain current with his or her publishing contacts. If an agent cannot contact publishers, then authors will not want to work with that person.

TOP FIVE QUESTIONS ABOUT BECOMING A LITERARY AGENT

1. *What skills will I need to develop to become an agent?*
   An agent should have excellent reading and comprehension skills, as well as negotiation, people, and time-management skills. More than any other skill, literary agents need self-direction and self-motivation. You have to be able to get out there and sell your author's book. You make money only when you sell.

2. *What type of education do I need to become an agent?*
   Most jobs in the publishing industry require or prefer a bachelor's degree in English or journalism.

3. *How do I decide which area to specialize in?*
   What types of books do you like to read? You don't have to work as an agent in the genre that you like the most, but it does help. Authors send material that matches an agency's focuses. That means you'll be reading a lot of one type of writing. It helps if you already have a passion for that genre and if you understand its market.

4. *How do I know whether I'm good enough to be an agent?*
   The world of a literary agent can be very high-pressure, as agents are always mindful of the fact that their clients are counting on them to sell their manuscripts. If you are comfortable with high-

Literary agents spend a lot of time working at a computer.

pressure situations, you might make a good agent. The other skills you need to become an agent, such as editing skills and being able to tell whether a manuscript will sell, can be learned more easily.

5. *What if I don't like to read?*

   If you dislike reading, working as a literary agent probably isn't the best job for you. However, there are many different types of agents. Within the publishing field, there are illustrator agents, who basically perform a similar service for artists. If you like art, this might be a good career choice for you!

Understanding which books sell is an important skill for a literary agent.

WOULD YOU MAKE A GOOD LITERARY AGENT?

So, would you like to become an agent? How do you know whether it is the right job for you? There are a few skills that can help you become a good literary agent.

EDITORIAL SKILLS

An agent should have strong editorial skills in order to help authors create the best books possible. Many agents first start out as editors. An editorial background helps them communicate to clients how exactly to make their books marketable. An agent also might check the manuscript for errors before sending it to a publisher. The competition to publish a book is very high, so the story needs to be perfect when the publisher reads it. If the publisher finds the story or concept weak, he or she will be unlikely to publish the book.

COMMUNICATION SKILLS

In addition to editorial skills, an agent needs very good communication skills. The agent must be able to communicate with the author and publishing company to secure the best deal for the author. Good negotiation skills are helpful, too. In most agencies, the agent gets paid on commission, so you want the best deal for your author as well!

KNOW THE MARKET

Since agents need to know the publishing market, most have a background in publishing. This provides them

FRIENDLY BUT TOUGH

Being friendly and having a great personality can be attractive in an agent. An author will want to continue working with you. But you also need to know when to be tough. Agents handle difficult negotiations, often regarding financial matters.

As a literary agent you will do a lot of reading, so loving to read is an important qualification.

industry insight. They make connections with editors, publishers, authors, and other professionals that will be useful when they become literary agents. An agent needs to know what kind of book will sell. This means you must keep track of current publishing trends by watching best-seller lists to see what people are reading. You will also need to keep track of market trends beyond publishing to help you predict what fad will hit the publishing industry next.

THE CHECKLIST

Still think this is the job for you? Answer the questions in the checklist to see whether you have what it takes to become an agent.

- *Do you like English or journalism?*

- *Are you good at negotiating?*

- *Are you good with people?*

- *Do you love to read?*

- *Do you keep up with current publishing trends?*

- *Do you have a strong background in computers?*

If you answered yes to most of these questions, you could be on your way to a career as an agent. But, even if you don't have the skills right now to become an agent, a little bit of hard work and determination will lead you on your way!

HOW TO GET THERE

WORK FOR THE WRITER

Authors have choices—if they don't like one agent, they can find another one. If you choose to be an agent, be sure to be polite, kind, and helpful to your clients. You are working for them.

CLASSES TO TAKE

For now, take writing and literature classes, as well as editing classes, if available at your high school. In college, you'll probably want to major in English or journalism. Business courses will also be helpful. You may want to seek out literary agents by e-mail and ask them what classes they took in high school and college.

KEEP READING

A love of all books is a must for a literary agent. You will need to identify a work's strengths and weaknesses and be able to tell the author your honest opinion of his or her work. This can be a fun but difficult task. Practice doing this with your friends and family. Have them write a story for you. Then, pretend they are authors who need you to critique their work. Ask them to give you feedback on how you handled the situation. Be open to their suggestions on how you can improve.

Continue to read as many books as possible. Read books that are top sellers or on the *New York Times* best-sellers list to give you an idea of what is popular in the current book market. It will be good practice for keeping up with the market when you become a literary agent. Reading many different kinds of books also can give you an idea of what type of authors you would like to represent as an agent. If you find that you enjoy a specific genre, you will want to find a job at an agency that publishes that type of book.

NETWORKING AND INTERNSHIPS

As an agent, you will go to writers' conferences, speak to groups of authors, and participate in other forms of networking to promote yourself. Before then, though, attend a writers' conference or seminar, and introduce yourself to any agents who may be there. Tell them you're interested in becoming an agent. Ask for business cards or their contact information. See whether they would be open to having you contact them with questions about the field.

SEPARATING GOOD FROM BAD

Being an agent means that you can tell whether a manuscript could turn into "the next big thing." But how can you develop this special skill? Find a local agent and ask whether he or she could be a mentor. Ask whether you could read a "bad" manuscript and a "good" manuscript. Why do you think each manuscript was labeled in such a way? Discuss your observations with your mentor.

Some larger literary agencies may offer internships or need readers to take a first pass at manuscripts. You'll have to give honest feedback on whether you think the manuscript would make a great book. Research local agencies in your

RESEARCH

It's not too early to start researching different publishing companies. You could create a list of companies and include what kind of books they publish, how many books they publish a year, and whom to contact. As an agent, you will need to know which publishing companies to approach with your clients' manuscripts. For example, if your client has written a young adult novel, you'll want to contact a publisher that has a reputation for publishing such works.

area. If there are none, see whether you can serve as a reader by e-mail. Before you know it, you could be on your way to a career as a literary agent!

A literary agent must develop strong negotiation skills
for dealing with publishers.

Travel writers get to see amazing places all over the world, such as the Taj Mahal in India.

WHAT IS A TRAVEL WRITER?

Before anything can be published, it has to be created. That's why publishers rely on writers to give them material to work with and, eventually, publish. Without writers, there wouldn't be anything to publish! There

74

are many different types of writers. Some publishers assign writers to a specific topic for an article or book. Other writers come up with their own ideas, write something, and try to sell it to a publisher.

Some writers only write about certain subjects or for a certain audience. One of the most adventurous types of writers is a travel writer!

Do you like variety? Do you want to see the world? Do you enjoy reading articles and books about traveling? Do you like looking at photos of faraway places? Maybe a career as a travel writer is for you. These writers travel all over the world and write about their experiences. They write about or review restaurants, culture, museums, and more. Some travel writers don't travel very far from home. They may do research into the best local places to visit with family or with pets.

Travel writers can work for themselves or for an organization, such as a newspaper, magazine, or travel book publisher. They may need to be willing to travel extensively, have new experiences, and participate in cultural activities that often greatly differ from what they are used to. Writing about their experiences is the number one requirement;

ADVENTURE STORIES

Some travel articles read like adventure stories. Travel writer Janet Fullwood has been publishing travel articles for more than 22 years. When asked what travel authors or books she reads or would recommend, she said, "Many, many—starting with [Rudyard] Kipling, Robert Louis Stevenson, Daniel Defoe, and other classic adventure writers."[1]

liking to travel is secondary. In other words, travel writers are writers first and travelers second.

Travel writers who work for book publishers, magazines, or newspapers are sent out on assignment to various places. In addition to assigning a deadline, the editor in charge will tell the travel writer what kind of story the publication is looking for—how long it should be and what kind of tone and focus it should have. For example, the editor may ask for a light piece about local food and culture, or a more in-depth look at a key site or museum, or even a piece on a certain exhibit, or an exploration of a remote area of natural beauty. A travel writer might also pitch an idea of a travel article to his or her publisher and write it if the publisher agrees. When writing about travel, he or she may use a first-person voice and make personal observations about the experience and recount anecdotes. No matter the story, a travel writer observes everything and talks to as many people as possible, often taking photographs along the way.

Sometimes a travel writer is paid to visit a site or specific hotel by a company that hopes to promote that vacation spot. A favorable article will help the hotel or destination bring in more customers. A free trip sounds great, but these types of assignments are usually the toughest for travel writers. During these trips, the travel writer has a busy itinerary with many interviews and meetings to attend. And since the writer is a guest, there is pressure to do and see everything the hosts want the writer to experience. Once the actual writing begins, the travel writer has to be careful. Was the experience genuine, or was it orchestrated to make

Rebecca Campbell is a 26-year-old travel writer
who took a 33-day trip around the world.

HOW DO YOU BOOK A TRIP?

When a travel writer gets an assignment, how does he or she work out the transportation to get there? Some freelance travel writers may work with a travel agent. Travel agents charge people a fee to help with their travel plans. Travel agents can book flights and hotel rooms and suggest places to visit. If the travel writer works for a publication, there may be people within that company who will help plan the trip.

sure the writer saw the trip in the best light possible? If the travel writer writes favorably, he or she needs to make sure the reporting is factual, too.

A travel writer may work on a freelance basis. In that case, the travel writer contacts various magazines, newspapers, or book publishers to see whether the publication has any available assignments. Sometimes the travel writer has to pay for the trip, or the publisher may reimburse the writer. One advantage to this arrangement is that the writer may be able to take on more than one assignment at a time. However, the travel writer will be responsible for paying his or her own taxes, and, usually, at least part of the travel expenses. Some people may start by working for a publication to gain experience; then, after a few years, they leave the company to become freelance travel writers.

No matter how they work, travel writers have to make sure their information is correct. People generally pay a good amount of money to go on a vacation. They do not want their vacation plans marred by an error in a guidebook or article. Including correct names and places is just the first, most obvious step in creating an accurate report. When writing about a place, such as a restaurant, museum, or amusement park, correct and up-to-date hours of operation are also key. Sometimes writers include specific, practical tips, such as the best time of day to visit a site or ways to avoid crowds or unnecessary expenses. Travel writers should double-check all of their facts before submitting an article.

GUIDEBOOKS

A guidebook can help plan a trip. Guidebooks tell about a certain city or country. They usually have lists of sites to see, places to visit, hotels to stay in, museums to check out, and restaurants to try. Each entry has a brief description. A guidebook might also include maps of the area or rating systems for the different locations. Some popular guidebook series include Lonely Planet, Let's Go!, and Frommers. Many guidebooks can be downloaded to devices such as the iPad or onto a cell phone so that people can easily access them while traveling.

WHAT IS A TRAVEL WRITER'S WORK ENVIRONMENT?

A travel writer's work environment is constantly changing because he or she is traveling a lot! Travel writers often stay in hotels when they research and write about the place they are visiting. A travel writer's tools need to be mobile—a laptop and small notebook are must-haves. This job requires the flexibility to work in a lot of different environments. In between working as a travel writer, most people need to take a second job to make ends meet. So, a travel writer must carefully schedule trips between periods of working at his or her other job.

HOW IS THE JOB MARKET FOR TRAVEL WRITERS?

It is not easy to find a job as a travel writer. There are not many jobs available, and the field is competitive. It is wise to start your travel-writing career by working for a publication if you can. Freelance travel writers often have a hard time earning a living without another job on the side. Travel writers who write as freelancers receive compensation for their articles based on length. The range for a 500-word article is $10 to $1,000, depending on the type of publication.[2] However, on average, travel writers are more likely to make between $25 and $300 per 500-word article.[3] If the travel writer authors a guidebook, the pay may be more substantial, but, again, it depends on the publishing company.

A PROFILE OF A TRAVEL WRITER

Freelance travel writer Michael Franklin has written travel articles for several magazines through the years. He loves writing travel articles because it gives him a chance to learn about new places, meet interesting people, and get out of his home office. Franklin says, "It's like work and a vacation at the same time."[4]

Travel writers check out attractions, such as restaurants, when they visit a place.

Franklin has a bachelor's degree in journalism and wrote for student publications while in high school and college. If you want to be a travel writer, Franklin believes, you should take a lot of English courses and learn how to write very well. He also suggests learning about the world by taking geography classes. If you have the opportunity to study abroad in college, Franklin says, "Go for it!"[5] He suggests writing an article about your trip for your school newspaper or Web site.

Franklin sometimes gets an idea for a travel article while he is traveling with friends and family. If he stumbles across a place that he thinks other travelers would like to know about and visit, he takes notes on it. When he gets back home, he can pitch his article idea to an editor. If the editor likes the idea, Franklin is contracted to write the article. Franklin also pitches ideas about places he hasn't visited yet, and sometimes publications come to him with their own trip ideas.

Franklin has an important insight for aspiring travel writers: "Blog about your adventures, or keep a journal. And remember, you can practice travel writing even if you don't travel."[6]

A DAY IN THE LIFE OF A TRAVEL WRITER

A travel writer's entire day may be spent getting to the destination he or she is going to write about! Other days might be spent looking for work. Still, a travel writer's day generally varies depending on whether he or she works for a publication or is a freelancer. If the writer works for a publication, he or she may attend meetings to brainstorm for the next travel article to write. If the writer is a freelancer, he or she may pitch ideas to magazines, newspapers, and blogs.

Once an idea is approved, the travel writer really gets busy. First, travel arrangements must be made. These may include flights, rental cars, and hotels. The writer will also research the destination as well as specific sites or relevant topics. He or she may schedule interviews, too.

TRAVEL AND THE ECONOMY

Travel writers should stay on top of the current travel trends. If the economy is weak, people may travel less but vacation locally instead. If this is the case, the travel writer will visit local attractions and write about those. A travel writer might also focus on destinations that offer discount deals.

When the travel writer reaches his or her destination, it's time to get to work! While traveling can be fun, the travel writer must do more research, conduct interviews, or tour the area for the article. The writer may also be responsible for taking photographs and providing descriptions of the photographs. Even while on a trip, the writer must be mindful of deadlines.

Having a background in photography can be helpful
to a travel writer.

TOP FIVE QUESTIONS ABOUT
BECOMING A TRAVEL WRITER

1. *What skills will I need to become a travel writer?*
   First, you need to know how to write. Other helpful
   skills include photography, travel experience, and a
   willingness to have new experiences. You also have

to be determined. It isn't easy to land a job as a travel writer!

2. *What type of education do I need?*
Travel writers could have bachelor's degrees in English or journalism. Learning foreign languages and geography classes could be helpful.

3. *When I'm working as a travel writer, will all of my expenses be paid?*
It depends. If you are writing for a very well-known publication, it is more likely that the destination will pay your way to garner good publicity. However, if you are writing for a lesser-known publication, you will probably need to pay your own expenses.

4. *How do I know whether I'm good enough to be a travel writer?*
Practice writing about places you find interesting. It could be the café down the street. See whether people like to read what you write. You really won't know whether you're good enough until you try it.

5. *How do I decide whether travel writing is right for me?*
Travel writing isn't for everyone. The travel writer will have to be away from home for short or long periods of time and may have to deal with travel delays and more. If you have always liked to travel and enjoy it, then travel writing may be a good choice for you. However, you must also like to write and share your travel experiences with others.

Travel writers must love to travel.

WOULD YOU MAKE A GOOD TRAVEL WRITER?

Are you interested in becoming a travel writer? Read on to see whether you have what it takes. You might be on your way to your dream job.

LOVE THE ROAD

First and foremost, travel writers should like to write about their adventures, and they should most certainly like to travel. Traveling can be fun, but it can also be taxing. There are many tasks a travel writer must undertake in order to prepare for a trip, such as researching an itinerary and making flight and accommodation reservations. Travel writing may sound like a lot of fun, but it's a lot of hard work, too. Travel writers must be prepared to work, not play, when they are on location.

If you're not sure if you like to travel, start locally. Spend a few hours touring your town, or take a day trip. If you can, travel to other states or to other countries with your family. Give travel writing a try. Take a notebook and a camera. Jot down notes of important things you want to remember to include in an article. Take photos so you can illustrate your article.

Regardless of where you start traveling, take notice of everything, and write your thoughts down. What do you see?

SPEAK THE LANGUAGE

Learning foreign languages may help you as you travel abroad. Even simply knowing key phrases such as "Where is the bathroom?" and "Where is the hotel?" will help you get around easier. You can find easy-to-use word and phrase books or even electronic translators, which look like small, handheld computers. You could also ask the people who work at the hotel where you're staying for help with key phrases and pronunciations.

What are the people like? What kinds of restaurants are nearby? Are there museums? Are there things for kids to do? For teens? For adults? Are there movie theaters? Are there shopping centers? What interests you when you're traveling?

WRITING SKILLS

Are you a good writer? If you don't have this skill yet, there is always time to learn. Travel writers should know how to write well. They must also be able to use different styles of writing. Some articles could have a personal, conversational tone—as if you were talking to a friend. Other articles may need to be more formal. Some articles also need to be purely factual. Other reviews can showcase the writer's opinion.

BE WILLING TO REVISE

Most travel writers submit their articles to editors at the publication they are working for. Sometimes, an editor will ask the travel writer to make changes to the article. Writers might not always like what editors have to say, but the editors know what their publication wants. As a travel writer, you'll need to be able to take criticism from an editor and revise your articles to make them even better. Keep in mind that the ultimate goal is to create the best article possible.

TRAVEL PHOTOGRAPHY

Can you take interesting photographs? Some publishers ask their travel writers to take photographs to go with the article they are writing. Some larger publications may send

Many travel writers enjoy the adventure of seeing new places.

a photographer along to a destination. Either way, it's a good idea to develop your skills—as well as your eye for what shots would best highlight an article.

CHECKLIST

Do you think you've got what it takes to become a travel writer? Answer the questions in the checklist below.

- *Do you like English or journalism classes?*

- *Are you a good writer?*

- *Do you like receiving feedback on your writing and revising it to make it even better?*

- *Do you like to travel?*

- *Are you good at photography?*

- *Can you meet tight deadlines?*

- *Do you like to meet new people?*

- *Do you study a foreign language?*

If you don't have these skills yet, it's okay! Even if you're not sure about traveling, start locally, and keep your travels simple. Start writing now. Everything takes time and practice. If you really want to be a travel writer, you can do it. Study hard, and learn all you can about travel writing.

HOW TO GET THERE

GET WRITING!

Learning to write well early will help you later on. While in high school, take writing classes. Ask your teachers about reference books that teach writing fundamentals. Writing reference books provide grammar, spelling, and punctuation rules. Writing for a school newspaper or magazine will also help you hone your writing skills.

Starting your own blog or keeping a journal will help you practice writing. If you wish to share your work, ask a friend or family member to review your article or story for grammar, spelling, and other errors. How can you make your writing more interesting? Are there any confusing parts? In what places does your story really come to life? Remember that your friend or family member is trying to help you write better, so don't get discouraged if they see errors or have questions. In fact, if they do see errors, consider it an opportunity to learn from your mistakes.

AVOID CLICHÉS

Be sure to avoid clichés in your writing. Clichés are overused expressions. They can make your writing seem amateurish and uninteresting. A few examples of clichés include: "fold under pressure," "you took the words right out of my mouth," or "whatever floats your boat."

LEARN ABOUT FARAWAY PLACES

If you're interested in traveling to certain areas abroad, learning the language may be a good idea. If your school doesn't offer that language, see

BE RESPECTFUL

One of the best ways to respect the people in the places you visit is to learn about cultural practices. In Japan, for example, the traditional greeting is a bow. Shaking hands is not common. You should also research an area's attire. For example, some countries require women to wear long pants or dresses and a head wrap.

Don't expect that everyone you meet when traveling can speak English. Learn how to ask, "Do you speak English?" in the native language or, better yet, learn the native language! Remember that no matter where you travel, you are representing your country and the publication you are writing for.

whether you can find computer programs or after-school programs that teach it.

Some high schools have foreign exchange student programs that allow you to spend a few weeks with a family in another country. This would be a great way to see whether you like traveling. It would also give you the chance to write about your experience. Wouldn't it be great to blog about your travels abroad? You could even add photos. Your friends and family would be able to read your blog back home.

Learn about other countries and their cultures, too. See whether you can find opportunities to travel with school groups or to study abroad in college. Ask your family whether you can host a foreign exchange student for a few weeks. These types of experiences help you learn about cultures that differ from your own. If you end up traveling to other countries as a travel writer, it will be helpful to understand that country's culture. It can save you from offending your hosts. The more you know about different cultures, the more prepared you'll be to travel to new and exciting places.

TAKE GOOD PICS

It is also a good idea to take a photography course. High schools and colleges may offer photography and other art classes that could be beneficial to the travel writer.

While you're out exploring your town, take photos. Practice with different angles, lighting, and shadows. Do you take neat, "artsy" shots, or do you like straightforward shots of particular subjects? It's fun to take a photograph and then write about why you took it and explain where you were.

AFTER HIGH SCHOOL

If you choose to be a travel writer and want to work for a publication, a bachelor's degree in journalism or English may be required. Even if you choose to become a freelance travel writer, a bachelor's degree may help you land assignments. Writing restaurant reviews or other travel pieces for your college's blog, newspaper, or magazine will help you gain valuable experience.

NATIONAL GEOGRAPHIC

National Geographic is one magazine that is full of travel articles and photographs. Purchase a copy or borrow the latest edition from your local library. Reading these articles will give you a good idea of what a travel article looks like. You will also learn about some exciting places you might want to visit.

NETWORKING AND INTERNSHIPS

Networking and internships can also be a great start into the travel-writing career. Ask your family and friends whether they are travel writers or know of any travel writers. These people may be able to give you some great advice on how to get started. They may also be able to help you obtain an internship.

Try looking for internships at newspapers and magazines. As an intern, you probably won't be traveling and might not even write much, but the experience will still help you learn about the industry.

BE PREPARED!

Are you ready for a trip across the country? Or even across the world? Do you have a passport yet? When you travel overseas or to other countries, you need a passport. Check with government Web sites, such as the US Department of State, for travel restrictions and other important information. These Web sites will also tell you exactly what you need to travel to another country and what you need to safely reenter the United States.

Do online research to find other travel writers. You may find blogs or Web sites with great tips. Don't be afraid to e-mail the travel writers. This would be a great opportunity to practice your interview skills. Introduce yourself in the e-mail as a student interested in learning more about travel writing. Keep your questions short and to the point. Be respectful when contacting travel writers, and thank them for their time. Remember, a travel writer might be busy and might not get back to you right away. Do not send multiple e-mails

Travel writers must always take notes
on their travel experiences.

unless the travel writer replies to your original message. If
you don't hear back, continue your online search for more
travel writers.

GET YOUR FOOT IN THE DOOR

N ow you know about some of the jobs in the publishing industry. You know what classes to consider taking in high school and college. You even have some tips to help you practice your new career. Getting a job is a lot more than practice and taking classes. You will have to go on interviews, and it helps to be prepared.

Interviewing skills are crucial—even for landing an internship. First impressions last a long a time. Go online, and research interview questions related to the job or career of your choosing. Then, ask a friend or family member to ask you the questions so you can practice answering them.

Job shadowing is another option. If the company you are contacting does not offer internships, ask whether you could shadow a magazine editor, book publisher, literary agent, or travel writer for a few days. That means you follow them around, take notes, and ask questions. This is a good way to make some connections in the publishing field. Job shadowing may also help you determine whether that particular career is for you.

Finally, you can always contact publishers and literary agencies to request more information about the industry. Be sure to ask clear, specific questions. You may not always hear back from the professionals you contact, but if you do, be sure to thank your contact for his or her time. If you plan on working in the field of publishing, you might be in contact with these people again. You want to maintain a friendly and professional relationship with them.

Breaking into the publishing industry will not be easy. No matter how excellent your skills, it may take some time to find a job in this highly competitive field. You may have several different internships before you find a full-time position, and every job you apply for is sure to have many interested applicants. Try not to get discouraged. If a job in publishing is your dream, it will be worth the work and wait to get there.

You could be on your way to a career in the publishing industry! Work hard, ask questions, and don't give up. Before you know it, you could be working at your dream job.

PROFESSIONAL ORGANIZATIONS

Here are some professional organizations you might want to contact for more information about the jobs in this book.

MAGAZINE EDITOR

American Society of Magazine Editors
www.magazine.org/asme

Canadian Society of Magazine Editors
www.canadianeditors.com

MPA: The Association of Magazine Media
www.magazine.org

BOOK PUBLISHER

Association of American Publishers
www.publishers.org

Independent Book Publishers Association
www.ibpa-online.org

Small Publishers Association of North America
www.spannet.org

LITERARY AGENT

Association of Authors' Agents
www.agentsassoc.co.uk

Association of Authors' Representatives
aaronline.org

TRAVEL WRITER

International Food, Wine & Travel Writers Association
www.ifwtwa.org

Midwest Travel Writers Association
www.mtwa.org

North American Travel Journalists Association
www.natja.org

Society of American Travel Writers
www.satw.org

MARKET FACTS

JOB	NUMBER OF JOBS	GROWTH RATE	
Editor	105,040	as fast as average	
Publisher	5,770	less than average	
Agent	7,500	less than average	
Writer	43,390	as fast as average	

ANNUAL MEDIAN WAGE	RELATED JOBS	SKILLS
$50,800	literary agent, writer, translator, proofreader, fact checker	competent with grammar, strong reader and writer, good communicator
$93,920	editor, literary agent	leader, good communicator, deadline conscious
$69,020	editor, modeling agent, acting agent	strong reader, experienced editor, great negotiator, confident
$53,900	reporter, news analyst, announcer, teacher, translator	creative, dedicated, willing to revise, open to new experiences

All statistics from the *Bureau of Labor Statistics Occupational Outlook Handbook, 2010–2011 Edition*

GLOSSARY

blog
An online journal.

brainstorm
To think up new ideas or solutions to problems quickly.

criticism
An in-depth analysis of something.

e-book
An electronic book read on a computer or e-reader.

editor
A person who reviews spelling, grammar, flow, and consistency within a newspaper, book, or article.

freelance
To work for several different companies instead of being permanently employed at a single company.

genre
A category of literature, such as detective novels or sci-fi books.

intern
Usually a high school or college student who works for a company without pay to learn about the business.

marketing

The act of promoting and selling a product or service.

negotiate

To reach an agreement through discussion.

page proofs

Preliminary version of a book meant for editing.

proofreader

A person who reads and marks corrections in proofs.

public relations

Communication by a person or organization with the purpose of creating a favorable public image.

reader

A person who reads manuscripts for agents.

ADDITIONAL RESOURCES

FURTHER READINGS

Adler, Jack. *Making Steady Money as a Travel Writer: Secrets of Selling Travel Stories—Without Traveling.* Bandon, OR: Reed, 2009. Print.

Allen, Moira Anderson. *Starting Your Career as a Freelance Writer.* New York: Allworth, 2003. Print.

Devantier, Alecia T., and Carol A. Turkington. *Extraordinary Jobs for Creative People.* New York: Ferguson, 2006. Print.

Kampmann, Eric M. *The Book Publishers Handbook: The Seven Keys to Publishing Success.* New York: Beaufort, 2007. Print.

Morrish, John. *Magazine Editing.* New York: Routledge, 2003. Print.

Parks, Peggy. *Writer.* San Diego, CA: KidHaven, 2004. Print.

Ventresca, Yvonne. *Careers for the Twenty-First Century: Publishing.* Farmington Hills, MI: Lucent, 2005. Print.

Zobel, Louise Purwin. *The Travel Writer's Handbook: How to Write-and Sell-Your Own Travel Experiences.* Chicago: Surrey, 2007. Print.

WEB LINKS

To learn more about publishing jobs, visit ABDO Publishing Company online at **www.abdopublishing.com**. Web sites about publishing jobs are featured on our Book Links page. These links are routinely monitored and updated to provide the most current information available.

SOURCE NOTES

CHAPTER 1. IS A PUBLISHING JOB FOR YOU?

1. "Hearst Magazine and Harpo Entertainment Group Announce Magazine Venture." *Hearst Corporation*. Hearst Communications, 16 Aug. 2010. Web. 8 July 1999.

2. Sam Harrison. *Ideaspotting: How to Find Your Next Great Idea*. Cincinnati, OH: F+W, 2006. Print. 15.

CHAPTER 2. WHAT IS A MAGAZINE EDITOR?

1. U.S. Bureau of Labor Statistics. "Authors, Writers, and Editors." *Occupational Outlook Handbook, 2010-11 Edition*. U.S. Bureau of Labor Statistics, 18 Feb. 2010. Web. 15 Sept. 2010.

2. Ibid.

3. U.S. Bureau of Labor Statistics. "Occupational Employment and Wages, May 2009: Editors." *Occupational Outlook Handbook, 2010-11 Edition*. U.S. Bureau of Labor Statistics, 14 May 2010. Web. 15 Sept. 2010.

4. Ibid.

5. Lisa Patterson. Message to the author. 11 Jul. 2010. E-mail.

6. Ibid.

7. Ibid.

8. U.S. Bureau of Labor Statistics. "Occupational Employment and Wages, May 2009: Editors." *Occupational Outlook Handbook, 2010-11 Edition*. U.S. Bureau of Labor Statistics, 14 May 2010. Web. 15 Sept. 2010.

CHAPTER 3. WOULD YOU MAKE A GOOD MAGAZINE EDITOR?

None.

CHAPTER 4. WHAT IS A BOOK PUBLISHER?

1. "Book Publisher." *Education-Portal.com*. Education-Portal.com, 2010. Web. 15 Sept. 2010.

2. Michelle Bisson. Message to the author. 12 Jul. 2010. E-mail.

3. Ibid.

4. Ibid.

5. "Book Publisher Salaries." *Simply Hired*. Simply Hired. 29. Sept. 2010. Web. 29 Sept. 2010.

CHAPTER 5. WOULD YOU MAKE A GOOD BOOK PUBLISHER?

None.

SOURCE NOTES CONTINUED

CHAPTER 6. WHAT IS A LITERARY AGENT?

1. Kelly Sonnack. Message to the author. 21 Jul. 2010. E-mail.

2. "Literary Agent Salaries." *Simply Hired*. Simply Hired. 29. Sept. 2010. Web. 29 Sept. 2010.

3. Ibid.

4. "Literary Agents." *Science Fiction & Fantasy Writers of America*. Science Fiction & Fantasy Writers of America, 18 Aug. 2010. Web. 29 Sept. 2010.

5. Andrea Brown. Message to the author. 13 Jul. 2010. E-mail.

6. Ibid.

7. Mary Kole. Message to the author. 16 Jul. 2010. E-mail.

8. Andrea Brown. Message to the author. 13 Jul. 2010. E-mail.

9. Ibid.

CHAPTER 7. WOULD YOU MAKE A GOOD LITERARY AGENT?

None.

CHAPTER 8. WHAT IS A TRAVEL WRITER?

1. "Janet Fullwood." *Rolf Pott's Vagabonding Update*. n.p., n.d. Web. 16 Aug. 2010.

2. Adam Williams. "What Does Travel Writing Pay?" *suite101.com*. Adam Williams, 17 July 2008. Web. 16 Aug. 2010.

3. Ibid.

4. Michael Franklin. Message to the author. 16 Jul. 2010. E-mail.

5. Ibid.

6. Ibid.

CHAPTER 9. WOULD YOU MAKE A GOOD TRAVEL WRITER?

None.

INDEX

ABOUT THE AUTHOR

Beth Townsend is a first-time author and has been an editor in the publishing field for over ten years. She encourages anyone who likes to read and who loves books to join the publishing field as she has.

PHOTO CREDITS